X-1

The Great Alphabet Race

by Janet & Roger Campbell

illustrated by Tom O'Sullivan

HAMLYN

LONDON · NEW YORK · SYDNEY · TORONTO

Published 1973 by
The Hamlyn Publishing Group Limited
London · New York · Sydney · Toronto
Hamlyn House, Feltham, Middlesex, England
by arrangement with Western Publishing Company, Inc.

ISBN 0 600 33929 7
Printed in Great Britain by Cox & Wyman Limited, London, Fakenham and Reading

It's the day of the Great Alphabet Race, and here in the kingdom of Zantippy, the excited citizens crowd into the seats near the starting line. The King has offered a prize of 100,000 gold pieces for the fastest means of transportation in the alphabet, and every rogue, rascal and scallywag in the kingdom has entered the race for the gold.

Just as the first rays of sun stream over the mountain tops, the starter fires his gun. They're off, on their race round the world!

But what's happened to Rollo Rhinoceros? Who put that hard-boiled egg in his rocket's fuel line? Poor Rollo. Now he'll never get off the ground. What can he do to get back in the race?

Aa

Air Ace Archie Anteater leads the race in the air, but his engine has flooded. He sputters down to an aircraft carrier for repair.

Bb

Baron Barnstorm Bear floats by in his balloon. He's so busy watching Archie through his binoculars that he doesn't see Rollo Rhino stowed away beside him. Rascally Rollo's boldly stealing a ride to the next town.

Cc

Carlo Cat cruises the overland route in his car. "The canoe," he purrs, "is for the canals of Venice. In canals I can't drive far."

Darlene's
Dumping
Inc.

Dd

Darlene Donkey's dumptruck deposits Rollo at the door of a shop. He needs a drill to clear the hard-boiled egg from his fuel line. Soon he'll have his rocket repaired.

Ee

Evan Engineer's engine screeches to a halt. "Eeek!" cries Evan. "Elephants eating eggs on the tracks!" He toots the whistle and clangs the bell but the elephants won't move. He'll just have to wait till the party's over.

Ff

Finally Rollo gets his rocket fixed. He lights the fuse and off he flies—right into a tree! What a flop. Farley Fox and his fire-engine crew stop long enough to put out the fizzling fire. This time, Rollo finds a gherkin in his steering gear. Sabotaged again!

Gg

Gwendolyn Goat gives Rollo a ride through Venice. They glide peacefully along the canals in her gondola. Suddenly . . .

Henrietta Hen hovers overhead in her helicopter. Help! She's kidnapping Rollo. Henrietta heads out to sea, but she runs out of fuel and has to make a forced landing . . .

Hh

Ii

. . . on an ice-breaker belonging to Captain Ichabod Iguana. Although they are icebound for several hours, the captain and crew pass the time ice-skating, until they can take Rollo to an airport in Iceland.

Jolly Rollo Rhino, now disguised as a reporter following the race, jumps into a Jaguar Airlines jet. Jojo Jaguar, stewardess, serves jam sandwiches and jasmine tea.

Jj

Kk

King Kenneth of Zantippy has entered the race, too. "I don't really want to give away all that gold," he explains, "so I'm hoping to win it myself." He's posted himself and his kayak by koala post to a nearby seaport.

Ll

Lettie Llama has landed her lunar module on the moon. ''You may think I'm a little off course,'' she says, strumming her lyre. ''Maybe I am. As a matter of fact, I think I'm lost.''

Mm

Meanwhile, Rollo, disguised as a myopic doctor, gets a ride on Murray Mandrill's motorcycle. "Well, if it's an emergency, Doc," says Murray, "just hop on." Murray didn't ask what kind of emergency. That was his mistake.

Nn

Now Rollo is underwater, because he needs to cross the channel. "I'm too heavy to swim on top," he explains. He quickly passes Norman Navigator, in his nautilus.

Oo

Over their heads, Admiral Octopus strides the deck of his ocean liner. "Full speed ahead," he orders, "or we'll be overtaken by pirates!"

Pp

Playing piano and piccolos, the musical pirates sail their pirate ship, singing:

"We once used to pillage,
But now we're too old,
If we win the race,
We'll retire with the gold."

PANDORA

Qq

The Queen of Quinstantinople needs a quartermaster for her quadruplane. Rollo gets the job. He climbs to the controls and quickly takes off.

X2

Rr

Rollo receives a parcel at his next stop. "It's my rocket!" he exclaims. "The repair shop posted it to me here. Now I'm really back in the race." He lights the fuse and roars away.

Ss

Sybil Sheep and her companions start at the South Pole and try to steal the lead by sliding on sledges all the way round the side of the world. Unfortunately, they soon run out of snow.

Tt

In Topeka, Rollo sells his rocket and takes a taxi. Suddenly a tram clatters past. It's Tandem Toad and his terrible troupe, tearing along the tracks toward victory.

Uu

Unfortunately the bridge road is unsafe, so Rollo rides a unicycle upon the railing. "Unbelievable," sings Ursula Bear, as she sails under the bridge.

Venture Van
Via
Cape Horn

Vv

Veronica Von Hippo rides in a van to Venezuela. She hopes to use the prize money of 100,000 gold pieces to buy a villa, and is taking all her furniture, just in case of victory.

Ww

A wretched Toucan has crashed into Carlo Cat. What a wreck! He arranges for Warren Walrus to haul the car to the finishing line with his wreckage-salvage lorry.

Xx

X marks the finishing line on the map, and the mysterious Mr X and his extraordinary crew sail their xebec toward the spot by way of Xanadu.

Yy

Yolanda Yak is so sure she will win that she stops her yellow yacht to celebrate. That's a mistake, because she hasn't won yet, and two contestants are nearing the finishing line.

YAKETY YA

Zz

Zarkof Zebra's zany zeppelin zigs and zags toward Zantippy. "It took a lot of sabotage, but at last I'm rid of that ridiculous Rhinoceros," he cries. "Quick, Zambisi, unzip the zeppelin—we must touch the ground to win."

The Great Alphabet Race is over! Zarkof has landed on the finishing line, but Rollo wins by a horn. The unhappy King has finished a poor third.

"Although I lost," he says, "and must give up my gold to Rollo, I decree that the entire prize must go toward a party for us all, to be held this very night in Zantippy Hall."

How Many of These Things Did You See in the Pictures?

In the picture of each letter, there are lots of things whose names start with that letter. Some are mentioned in the text and some aren't, but they're all listed below. How many did you find?

Did you notice the International Alphabet Code Flags in the pictures? There's a different flag for each letter of the alphabet. These flags are used all over the world to send messages from ship to ship.

aeroplane
anteater
angler fish (*on plane's wing*)
algae
anchor (*on plane's tail fin*)
aircraft-carrier
American flag
albatross

balloon
bear
binoculars
basket
bicycle
bows
bee (*on the flag*)
bananas
bull
ball
beetle (*above the bull*)

car
cat
condor
canoe
crocodile
cardinal
crab
crab cage

dumptruck
donkeys
door
dog
duck
ducklings

engine
eagle
engineer's hat
eight
elephants
emperor's wreath
Empire sofa
eggs
eggcups

fire-engine
foxes
firemen
frog
fuses (*on Rollo's rocket*)

gondola
goat
gull

helicopter
hen
hats
hamster
herons (*under the gondola's canopy*)
horns (*on Gwendolyn Goat's head and Rollo's nose*)

icebreaker
iguanas
"Icarus"
ice
ice skates

jet
jaguar
jam sandwiches
journalist
jack rabbits
jet engine

kayak
king
kingfishers
kiwi
kettle
knight (*chess piece*)
koalas
kazoo
knot

lunar module
llama
lyre

motorcycle
mandrill baboon
mechanical mandarin duck
melons
moustache
mackerel (*in Rollo's pocket*)
magpie (*on Rollo's hat*)